YOUR KNOWLEDGE HAS VALUE

Sabrina Habermann

British Cultural Studies: An Overview

GRIN Verlag

Bibliografische Information der Deutschen Nationalbibliothek:

Die Deutsche Bibliothek verzeichnet diese Publikation in der Deutschen National-
bibliografie; detaillierte bibliografische Daten sind im Internet über http://dnb.d-
nb.de/ abrufbar.

Imprint:

Copyright © 2010 GRIN Verlag GmbH
Druck und Bindung: Books on Demand GmbH, Norderstedt Germany
ISBN: 978-3-656-53227-9

This book at GRIN:

http://www.grin.com/en/e-book/263611/british-cultural-studies-an-overview

GRIN - Your knowledge has value

Der GRIN Verlag publiziert seit 1998 wissenschaftliche Arbeiten von Studenten, Hochschullehrern und anderen Akademikern als eBook und gedrucktes Buch. Die Verlagswebsite www.grin.com ist die ideale Plattform zur Veröffentlichung von Hausarbeiten, Abschlussarbeiten, wissenschaftlichen Aufsätzen, Dissertationen und Fachbüchern.

Visit us on the internet:

http://www.grin.com/

http://www.facebook.com/grincom

http://www.twitter.com/grin_com

British Cultural Studies

Sabrina Habermann

Pädagogische Hochschule Heidelberg
British Cultural Studies, winter semester 2009
March 31, 2010

Table of Contents

1.   Own discussion and analysis of the term "culture"

A large number of people believe that everything that is man - made can be seen as culture. Moran leaves no doubt about those products' importance, when he writes: "Products, the visible dimension of culture, are the gateway to the new culture, the new way of life" (p. 48). But are there only architecture, paintings, literature, music, language, and food which come to mind if we think of a country's culture? The iceberg model shows that these aspects represent only a small amount of culture that, just like the visible section of an iceberg above the waterline, can be seen easily and understood clearly. However, there are a lot more facets, also like an iceberg, that can only be suspected or imagined. These parts of the iceberg are its foundation and the iceberg model makes clear that it is impossible to understand people from different cultural backgrounds, unless we are able to appreciate what the foundations of their culture are. But no matter how many different definitions of the term "culture" exist, a lot of them cover problems concerning the human beings and their life in a community. This implies that we can't learn about another country's culture by reading a lot of books about it, but we need the encounter with another way of life. In that way, culture can also be seen as a concept which regulates the interpersonal cohabitation of human beings in a collective. This collective does not have to be a country by all means, but can also be a group of people with the same interests. If some people who are fond of a special musical genre such as goth, pool together, they have their own culture, too and it is not necessary that they live in the same country. But it is not merely the music that connects them, but rather "shared interpretations about beliefs, values, and norms, which affect the behaviors" (Lustig, Koester, 2003, p. 27) and influence the way their thinking is organized.

As well as from different communities, such values and norms can also be passed from one generation to another. Especially views about the importance of time, concepts of beauty, child raising beliefs, and rules of social etiquette can differ from one culture to another and are interpreted differently. If a foreigner does not know this other view of the world, it is sometimes very difficult for him to become part of the new culture. Consequently it is essential that we become clear that it is impossible to understand another country's culture if we only try to build our cultural understanding on our own view of the world and stereotypical perceptions. Confucians say that "Human beings draw close to one another by their common nature, but habits and customs keep them apart". To solve this problem, the main point is to be open - minded and to accept other countries' attitudes.

2.   The United Kingdom - four countries or only one

The consideration of the term culture is also an important one if we think about the United Kingdom. As the name implies it is a union between four countries that are England, Northern Ireland, Scotland, and Wales. But why do the Scots and the Welsh as well as the people from Northern Ireland often define themselves in terms of their individual nationalities, rather than as British?

Different Roots

Perhaps the answer can be found in the British Isles' history. Oakland makes clear that there was a big wave of immigration in former times because it was relatively easy to get free access to Britain. Due to this fact, the people who live in Britain nowadays have different roots from all over the world (2006, p. 69). Brisk argues that "one's history is defined not only by where one was born and where one grew up but also by the history of one's ancestors" (2008, p. 36). As a consequence the people from Wales, Scotland, and Northern Ireland have indeed the same language, but different accents and disparate values and norms of which they are proud. This is mainly the case because they make them unique and only in that way they are able to contrast themselves from England and forget "England's hegemony over the rest of the British Isles" (Morley, Robins, 2001, p. 41). Furthermore ethnic minorities such as Black Caribbeans, Pakistanis or Bangladeshis came to Britain a long time ago and some of them retained their own culture, as well (Oakland, 2006, p. 52). They are all proud of what they are and their heritage.
So there has always been a difference between the people of the British Isles.

Britishness

But then what about the term "Britishness"? Is it a term with no meaning? As I said, there are a lot of differences among the British Isles' population, but in his speech in 2007 Gordon Brown, Great Britain's Prime Minister, pointed out that despite some cultural differences, there is also a common culture which is shared by the whole population of Great Britain. He gave points to his words when he said: "Britain has something to say to the rest of the world about the values of freedom, democracy and the dignity of the people that you stand up for." It sounds good, but in my opinion it is only a constructed Britishness because a lot of other countries have the same values about freedom and dignity as well and they are not British either. Britishness today is a vague term and almost only used for political reasons.

A Political Union

Maybe Great Britain's politics is one of the few things all inhabitants of Briton really have in common.

On the one hand, Britain is a constitutional monarchy which means that the Queen is head of England, Wales, Scotland and Northern Ireland and reigns "without executive powers under constitutional limitations" (Oakland, 2006, p. 86) at the same time. Additionally each of the four countries is governed by the UK Parliament and the UK government in many areas. On the other hand Delanoy and Volkmann highlighted that some political changes, especially those in 1998, caused questions about what holds Britain together. (2006, p. 38). It is a justified question because due to the devolution of parliaments for Wales, Scotland, and Northern Ireland in 1998, these countries can decide about affairs like "education, health, transport, environment, home affairs and local government", on their own (Oakland, 2006, p.84). This means that even in the politics there are very few things left that accomplish a connection between the UK's four countries.

Conclusion

In my opinion the UK can rather be seen as four countries than as one. Each citizen of the UK has indeed a British citizenship, but this does not mean that they have a British identity as well. In most instances the English, Welsh, Scottish, and Northern Irish people are of the opinion that they have different cultural and national identities mainly because their ancestors developed their own customs and their own way of life. Today these differences keep them apart and make four countries out of a former union. The few similarities,the four countries have in common, like the same language or the same head of state cannot help to reunite them due to the fact that the UK's inhabitants are highly aware of their differences.

3.   Television in Britain

In the UK, like in a lot of other countries, television has become an important part of people's everyday life. As a result, 98 per cent of the population have TV sets and the average television viewing time per week in the UK is about 25 hours (Oakland, 2006, p. 245). It is not the news reports or documentaries that attract the viewers' attention, but it is soap operas that appeal the mass.

The question is, why especially these programs, which are sometimes of a low quality and with a high amount of sex and vulgarity, are watched by millions of people every day.

The Soap Operas' Popularity

Maybe a lot of people are of the opinion that it is the stories' open – ended nature, which makes the viewer switch on the TV day after day, but the statement that those series live particularly by their alertness to what is happening in culture (Morley & Robins, 2001, p. 262) is a more suitable one if we talk about the soap operas' popularity because only if people are able to identify themselves with the soaps' characters, they are going to watch them day by day.

EastEnders

The soap opera EastEnders is a good example for a soap opera which is designed in a way that suits a wide range of the UK's inhabitants with different cultural backgrounds and different nationalities. It is not for nothing that EastEnders is one of the most popular soaps in the UK. "It projects out to the widest edges of the culture its own mix of original and reworked cultural experience (attitudes, jokes, styles, personalities, looks, situations, types, ways of speaking)" (Morley & Robins, 2001, p. 262).

The Setting

One of the reasons why EastEnders seems so realistic to the people is the setting. The story is set in Walford, a fictitious neighbourhood of London's East – End. Most of the characters are living and working in Albert Square. The fact that the soap's characters live in ordinary houses and go shopping in small greengrocer's shops creates a connection between the soap and the viewers' every day.

British Social Realism

But more than the setting, it is the presentation of ordinary life on TV which is fascinating for the viewers. EastEnders is about neighbourhood – relationships, relationships within the family but also about people of a working – class community who are not very successful in their lives. Problems are presented which could happen to anyone of the viewers anytime, so that they tend to laugh with the characters as well as cry with them. For a lot of British people solidarity in the family is also an important issue which is taken up in this soap because most of the characters are related to each other and each of them has a place in the community. Morley and Robins leave no doubt about the importance of the term community in soap operas when they write that soaps "have to be understood in terms of a particular, national version of community. This version is grounded in a broad set of cultural meanings surrounding locality, social class, wealth, and family" (2001, p. 266). Storylines including violence, rape, murder and child abuse help to create a series which is true – to – life.

Cast And Characters

But the main reason EastEnders is so popular in the UK and attracts the attention of the mass is the "culturally diverse cast" (Aron & Livingstone). There are black, Asian, Turkish and Polish characters. This cast represents the British multi – ethnic society and therefore even British immigrants have the possibility of identification with some characters (Aron & Livingstone). But there are not only people from other countries playing an important role in the soap, but also ill and disabled people.
In that way the soap opera EastEnders is true – to – life and that is why it is so popular in the UK, as well as in a lot of other countries.

4.   Developing Cultural Awareness

Teaching culture in a foreign language classroom is not as easy as it sounds. The question is how to teach it in a way that students become open – minded to a foreign culture and are able to abandon their stereotypes about this country.
In his book "Introduction to English Language Teaching" Andreas Müller – Hartmann points out that teaching the foreign countries' policies and history is not enough to develop students' cultural awareness (2001, p. 110). So teachers have to find some cultural aspects which create a connection between the children's world and the foreign culture.

Teaching Unit On Notting Hill Carnival

Now I would like to introduce some ideas for a teaching unit on Notting Hill Carnival. I have chosen this part of British culture because carnival is an event known by every child in Germany and it shows clearly that Great Britain is a multi – ethnic society. Additionally it helps the children to give up the stereotype that Britons are reserved, when they see a lot of them celebrating on the streets.

The Beginning

At the beginning the children are asked to have a look at this picture.

http://clubbingwith cherrywilson. files.wordpress. com/2009/08/ notting-hill. jpg (24.03.10)

Along with it, they can hear a song from Notting Hill Carnival. After having had a look at the picture, they shall describe what they can see in it (colours, how the people look like or their skin colour), but also guess in which country the scene could have taken place and which atmosphere the picture reflects. Additionally they should think about how the people in this picture feel.

Through this event which is also very popular in Germany, it is easier for the students to create a connection to their experience realm and to awake their interest.

Collecting Previous Knowledge

After the picture's description the term "German Carnival" is being written in the middle of the board. The teacher explains that the students should write everything they know about German Carnival on the board. The requirement is that there cannot be more than three people at the board at the same time and nobody is allowed to talk.

Through this method, the teacher is able to find out how much previous knowledge the students have about carnival. Later on, it is easier for the pupils to find out about German and Notting Hill Carnival's differences and similarities.

Groupwork

Subsequently, the students are divided into four groups. Each of them gets information about a specific part of Notting Hill Carnival. Based on this information they should make informative posters in teamwork.

Group 1: History

Group 2: Food

Group 3: Music

Group 4: Ethnic Minorities

Gallery Walk

After the completion the pupils are asked to make a Gallery Walk. This means that each group shows its result on a special place in the classroom. One of the group's members is standing at this place and is available for the gallery visitors' questions. All the other members of the group are changing stations every five minutes. In that way each student knows about each important part of Notting Hill Carnival after the Gallery Walk.

Discussion With A Partner

At least the students should talk about the parts the German and the Notting Hill Carnival have in common and about the parts in which they differ from each other, with a partner. In that way it may be that they neglect their stereotypes about the UK because they have found out in the teaching unit that Britain is a multi – ethnic society with a lot of colourful facets and different nationalities. Additionally it should have become clear that British people are not that different from Germans and not boring or reserved by all means.

References

Aron & Livingstone. Retrieved March, 15, 2010 from The Museum of Broadcast
Communications
   http://www.museum.tv/eotvsection.phpentrycode=eastenders

Brisk, M. (2008). Language, Culture, and Community in Teacher
   Education. Taylor & Francis Group, LLC

Brown, G. (2006). Retrieved March, 20, 2010 from Wikipedia
   http://en.wikipedia.org/wiki/Britishness

Delanoy & Volkmann (2006). Cultural Studies in the EFL
   classroom. Heidelberg: Universitätsverlag Winter

Lustig & Koester (2003). Intercultural Competence:
   Interpersonal communication across cultures.

Moran, P. (2001). Teaching Culture. Perspectives in
   Practice. Heinle & Heinle

Oakland, J .(2006). British Civilization. An Introduction.
   Routledge

Müller – Hartmann, A.(2007). Introduction to English Language
   Teaching. Stuttgart: Klett

Morley & Robins (2001). Cultural Studies. New York: Oxford
   University Press